Copyright © 2025 Katherine Flynn. All rights reserved.

No part of this workbook may be reproduced or transmitted in any form or by any means—electronic, mechanical, photocopying, recording, or otherwise—without prior written permission from the author, except for brief quotations in reviews or educational use.

This workbook is intended for personal growth, reflection, and spiritual exploration. It is not a substitute for professional medical, psychological, or legal advice. The author disclaims any liability for the use or misuse of the material contained herein.

Portions of the imagery and design elements are used under license from Creative Fabrica. Guided by the wisdom of the Druids and the elements, this work is offered for your personal journey. Please honor the integrity of this material by not reproducing or distributing it without permission.

www.thechanneledsource.com

I'm excited you've taken this next step to find and live your passion and purpose! Let me tell you, I've been there before, and after my long journey of finding not only who I am, but my purpose and reason for incarnating I am now supporting others to find theirs.

Through my ability to connect with Source, energy and experiences, I'm excited to support you on your journey of uncovering your life purpose and passion for life! We will take this one step at a time, and allow your soul to lead the way!

This workbook will allow you to reflect on many parts of your life, knowing that some will change, while others will just need to be slightly adjusted. Allow for your soul to lead the way and don't over think your answers. Each week you will reflect back on what has happened and make any changes needed.

Each of these modules connects to the energy of an element. These allow you to look at each part of your life in a way that can reconnect you with your soul and purpose. I'd recommend spending a week on each section. That will give you time to contemplate and sit with the topic of the week before moving on.

Try not to over think each section, and allow the energy to encompass you. If you are working with water and feel a little more emotional, give yourself the grace to work through the energy and either integrate, transmute or release it.

Growth takes time, and the same way we allow a flower to take time to blossom, give yourself the same time. I have faith in your ability to transform yourself in any area you are focusing on. Have your intention ready as you begin next step to live to your highest purpose.

-Katherine

Uncovering Your Life Purpose

Uncovering your life purpose is the key to living an extraordinary life.

Every human life is full of twists and turns, ups and downs, observation and learning. Aligning your life with your highest purpose is the key to finding contentment, peace and joy along the way. We help you explore your life purpose and map out your path so that you can live the the centered, peaceful and dynamic existence that you came here to live.

When you combine your powerful soul with positive intention and faith in a great being, everything is possible. The point of life is to expand. By embracing the knowledge Source can provide, you can build the life you came here to live, and expand in all the ways you need to for your soul's growth.

What you find may surprise you, but don't get discouraged, for some uncovering your life purpose may take several months or even years. Don't get frustrated, you will know when you have found your true path, so if it takes a while, enjoy the ride!

Using this Workbook

Each section is meant to give you time to reflect on a certain part of your life and those aspects in it. These are just recommendations on how to use the workbook, but you can do what feels best for you.

Recommendations:
1. Take 1 week for each element, but feel free to take more time if needed.
2. Reflect back through the pages of your current element and make additions as necessary.
3. Complete the reflection page on the same day you start the next element.
4. If you need another journal, to write it down, feel free, you don't have to fill all the space, or fit your answer into the space.
5. Allow yourself to let other thoughts or ideas come through, even if they are not part of the question or topic. There is a reason they are coming up, so let them flow and see where it takes you!

Reflection Page

Reflect on where you have been and where you want to go. Do not limit yourself, but let your mind, intuition and soul speak on this page. Write down any learnings, energy, experiences, etc.

Workbook Intention

Reflect on your intention including the energy and feelings around it. Some questions to get you started: What is your intention for completing this workbook? What was the reason you are here? Where do you feel an imbalance in life?

 # Connection to the Elements

The element of earth provide us with the energy to truly transform. When you work with each of the elements, individually it shows you a different aspect of the energy, experience or opportunity to grow.

By combining the energies of each of the elements, you're able to focus on the transformation you are seeking, and it is exponentially powerful. Each element shows us a different aspect of source energy which allows for the energy to flow and show you how to transform. Remember that you are the creator of your own destiny and anything is possible!

- Earth — *Grounding*
- Water — *Emotions*
- Air — *Life Force*
- Fire — *Transformation*
- Celestial — *Source Connection*

Transformational Energy

Earth *Grounding and Foundation*

Creating a Plan: Uncover your foundation including the obstacles you are facing, potential healing, and what you have already uncovered through other modalities. We will take a deeper look at where you've been, are currently, where you want to be.

Water *Energy, Emotion, and Intuition*

Energies: Dig deep into the energies around you and how your emotions, intuition and past experiences have shaped you into the person you currently are.

Air *Balance, Harmony and Connection to Life Force*

Career & Hobbies: The way we spend our time can either bring us joy, or tribulations. Balance and harmony in these areas can allow us to maintain/increase our power, vibration and presence. When our energy is balanced, it allows us feel aligned and fulfilled and drives our life force energy.

Fire *Will Power, Inner Strength, Transformation through Action*

Bringing it Together: You are limitless when you combine your powerful soul with positive intention. This week we will bring all of the work you have done in previous weeks together to have a plan of action that is life-changing.

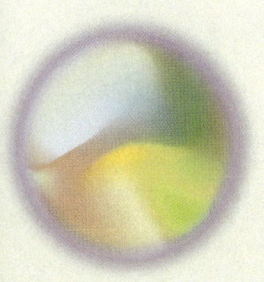

Celestial *Connection to Source, Authenticity*

Going forward: This week you will review the integration of the plan that we created to see how it is flowing in your life to live the life you came here to live.

Elements and You

How do you connect to the elements? Think of all of the times where you were needed to ground, calm down, bring up your energy or center yourself?

Earth
Grounding and Foundation

As Spiritual people, we always think of ourselves as celestial spiritual beings, which we are. But that is only part of it. In truth, we are also from the earth. The bodies our soul's incarnate in are truly the earth, and the grounding and foundational energy it provides for us allows us to experience life in a way that can not be done otherwise. For when you look at something through the human perspective, it is seen in a way no other being or energy can.

Mother Earth provides all we need for living the life that each soul came here to live. Through food, shelter, medicine, heat, breath, etc, all of these are resources on the earth and gifts that Mother Earth has given to us. It's important to utilize them, and connect back to her when we are in times of need, stress, anxiety or any obstacle or time of need that comes up. She is our foundation, and has the resources to connect us back to our earthly roots. When our foundation is not solid, it's time to relook at what makes us who we are. All we need to do is look, and trust as Earth and the Universe will always show us exactly what we need.

Foundation

Now it's time to look at what makes you who you are your core. Write down, what makes you the person you are. Beliefs, Family, Friends, Morals, etc. If you have to describe yourself to someone, what would you say? Don't judge yourself, be truly honest.

Joy & Passions

Recognizing your passions is one of the first steps to finding your life purpose and path, and grounding to what drives you in this lifetime. When we do or experience something that brings us joy, it is our soul's way of showing us our path.

Take some time to think about what you enjoy and love. Even the smallest thing is important, so note them below. Here are some questions to start you.
- What drives you and brings passion to your life?
- What do you enjoy?
- What brings a smile or laugh to you?

Foundation & Joy

Spend some time reflecting on the last 2 exercises.

Where are the similarities and differences?
How do they connect?

Don't sensor what you write, just let it flow!

Obstacles

What obstacles do you feel are in your way? Ex: foundation, money, support, safety, trust, health, etc.

What beliefs do you have around these obstacles?

Direction/Intention

Based on everything reviewed and discussed during the Earth section where do you see, has anything changed?

Week's Focus

List 3 things that you will focus on for this week that will support the direction you want to go in life. The things you will do everyday to support your intention.

Reflection Page

Before Water, think back to the last week and what energies, triggers, and experiences the universe has given and shown you. Any revelations, triggers, or transformations?

Water
Energy, Emotion and Intuition

Water is the life force within all beings and comes in many forms. It is an element of emotion and deep contemplation. It allows beings to look within and find those triggers, beliefs and energies that do not serve any longer. Water then allows for cleansing and purification, to make us anew.

It gives and sustains life in many forms. It's important to go back to water when you need revitalization and clearing. This provides an opening for you to adjust the energies in your life, let your emotions flow, and feel the cleansing that is so important. Through doing this you connect to your intuition and allow your soul to support you on your journey.

Triggers

When triggers show themselves, it's our soul's way to bringing something to the surface that we need to look at to either transform, release or even just recognize the learning.

What as the main trigger you experienced? What did it bring up? A memory, feeling, belief, etc? How did you work with it?

Energies

All of our experiences, people we meet even situations create energy. Everything is energy, and we can feel it as a force is many different ways. These can come up with feelings, thoughts or sensations. What comes up for you could come from either new, current or past energies.

What do you think of when you think of energies around you? Are they good or bad? Does it connect to a experience or person?

Connection

What similarities do you find between the energies you felt and your triggers? How are they connected?

What do these connections mean to you? How do they align to your life? Do they help or hinder you finding joy everyday? How could you align them to find joy?

Beliefs and Programs

Everyone comes in with beliefs and programs that are set from past lives, ancestral energy, or during our childhood. Based on your triggers, what beliefs and programs are coming to light? What is an aspect you want to keep, and what are you ready to release? Think of as many as you can and reflect on what each means to you and your life.

Review

What do you want to keep with you? What resonates with to who you truly are and who you want to be?

How can you do things differently to find joy and your purpose?

Direction/Intention

Based on everything reviewed and discussed during the Earth and Water section, has anything changed or transformed? Restate your intention.

Week's Focus

List 3 things that you will focus on for this week that will support the direction you want to go.

Reflection Page

Think back to the last week and what energies, triggers, and experiences the universe has given and shown you this past week. Any revelations, or transformations?

Air

Balance, Harmony and Connection to Life Force

Air is the life force of earth and everything on it! Air can calm, restore, build, create or even restrict. Without realizing, we connect to the energy of air every single moment of the day. It provides us life through breath, brings to us what we need, or removes what we do not. It is the most precious of gifts that earth provides, in addition to supporting the other elements.

As you sit and feel it on your body, know it is the energy of Mother Earth moving over every living thing. It is as it should be and allows for each living organism to bring with it what it needs to survive. Just as we need air to live, our lives need balance in work, family, friends, and hobbies.

The energy of Air brings balance to each of us, along with the other elements to move forward on the journey of life.

Balance

It's important to have balance in your life to balance out all that comes to you. Without it your energetic alignment and life purpose will not feel center or that you are on your path.

Reflect on where you have balance. Is there an area of your life which feels incomplete or too much of a focus?

Who are you when you are out of balance? What traits or energies do you show?

Harmony

Just like balance, you need harmony as well. How would you describe Harmony? How is this shown in your life, or now is it not?

Are there areas where you aren't feeling harmonious? How does this affect your mood?

Balance & Harmony

How do these two show similarities and differences?
What "aha's" are coming up?

Who are you when you are out of balance and harmony? Who would you like to be when in are in and out of balance and harmony?

How do you think you can live a more balanced lifestyle?

Life Force

How do these things bring your life into focus, or make you get out of bed everyday. What is it that drives you?

How can you implement the things that drive you into your life everyday?

How do the things that bring out your life force energy connect to your passions and joy in your life? What commonalities are you seeing from the past elements?

Do you need to implement or change anything to live in joy on your path? If so, what is that?

Direction/Intention

You should have a very good idea of the steps you need to take to walk in your purpose and on your path. If you would like to fine tune it, please do so!

Week's Focus

List 3 things that you will focus on for this week that will support you in reaching and living in your purpose.

Reflection Page

Think back to the last week and what has the universe has given and shown you this past week. Any revelations, triggers, or transformations? How are you finding more direction and purpose in life?

Fire

Will Power, Inner Strength, and Transformation

Fire provides humans with warmth, light and purification. The energy it provides is equally strong to others but has a greater sensation to humans. It can purify anything and allows new growth to form as it is the element of new birth. This can be done through burning away part of the land all the way to how a candle removes negative energy. When revered and honored, it can provide so much to the human life.

Fire is the element of transformation, allowing for you to have a death and rebirth of a new part of your life. Whether it be small, or large, each transformation is a step towards living in Joy, Happiness, and your Life Purpose.

Areas of Transformation

Looking back at the last 3 elements, what areas have already started to transform? Has it been your attitude, energy, vibration, or something tangible such as a new hobby, or routine? How have you integrated each week's energies?

Challenges to Transformation

Is there anything getting in the way? What energies, beliefs, programs or blocks are coming forward? Have you shifted them prior, and now they are coming back, or have they never left? What are ways you can transform, integrate or realign?

Renew

Recognition of the energies, routines, and beliefs that either help or hinder us allows us to let go of what no longer serves us and renew ourselves to our purpose and higher power. How do you want implement these new transformative energies and actions? What has already naturally happened to align them?

Rebirth

Looking back, how have you implemented the focuses from the last 3 sections? Where are you feeling yourself change and transform? What areas do you still feel unbalanced?

Reflection Page

Think back to the last week, how have you embraced change? What resonates with you, and what still feels uncomfortable?

Celestial
Connection to Source & Authenticity

All life forms are from the planet, but the souls and essences come from the celestial realm, which can also be known as Source, God, The Universe, etc. This energy and space are always with us and allows a reconnection back to where all beings are from.

Each of the elements is part of Source and allows us to see an aspect of the universal energy, but when they are all together, we can see how Source energy can bring everything together. Trust in yourself, knowing your soul, guides and all celestial beings will assist you to live your exceptional life!

Reflection Page

You have now completed all 5 elements, and are in such a different, more aligned place in your life. Look back on where you came from, where you are and where you still would like to go.

Take credit for all of the work you have done, and let's celebrate!

Remember, our growth never ends, but as you have become more aware of triggers, emotions and energies, you can continue to live your life purpose in true alignment to source!

Moving Forward

In what ways will you continue your journey of transformation and aligning to your life purpose? Is there anything that still feels misaligned?

How will you work with it?

Congratulations on completing the Align to Your Life Purpose workbook! Your dedication and hard work have brought you to this milestone, and you should be incredibly proud of yourself. Remember, this is just one step in your ongoing journey of growth, learning and expansion.

The skills and knowledge you've gained here are invaluable tools that you can continue to build upon. Keep pushing forward, stay curious, and don't hesitate to dive into new energies, triggers or unbalances.

The process you used can be utilized again and again, and you may find that each time it gets simpler as the energy shifts more quickly.

Your potential is limitless, and every effort you make brings you closer to your goals and the alignment to your life purpose.

Enjoy these moment and the ride as you continue to align to your life's purpose.

-Katherine

Made in the USA
Coppell, TX
08 January 2026

68528442R10029